Debths

Books by Susan Howe
Available from New Directions

The Birth-Mark

The Europe of Trusts

Frame Structures: Early Poems 1974-1979

The Midnight

My Emily Dickinson

The Nonconformist's Memorial

Pierce-Arrow

The Quarry

Sorting Facts: or, Nineteen Ways of Looking at Marker

Souls of the Labadie Tract

Spontaneous Particulars

That This

Debths

Susan Howe

A New Directions Paperbook Original

PUBLISHER'S NOTE: *Woodslippercounterclatter*, a collaborative performance by Susan Howe and the composer David Grubbs, was produced as a CD in 2014 by Blue Chopsticks, under the Drag City label. Parts of *Tom Tit Tot* appeared in *Woodslippercounterclatter* and also were exhibited at Yale Union in Portland, Oregon, and in the Whitney Biennial of 2014. Portions of *Debths* have appeared in *Hambone* and in the *Cambridge Literary Review*.

AUTHOR'S NOTE: Grateful acknowledgment is made to the Isabella Stewart Gardner Museum Archives; *New Poems, Manuscript Materials* by W. B. Yeats (edited by J.C.C. Mays and Stephen Parrish, Cornell University Press); *The Collected Works of Samuel Taylor Coleridge, Vol. 16, Part 2: Poetical Works II: Poems (Variorum Text)* (edited by J.C.C. Mays, Princeton University Press); and *Paul Thek: Diver, a Retrospective* by Elisabeth Sussman and Lynn Zelevansky, with essays by George Baker (Whitney Museum of American Art and Carnegie Museum of Art, Yale University Press).

Design by Leslie Miller
Manufactured in the United States of America
First published as New Directions Paperbook 1380 in 2017

Library of Congress Cataloging-in-Publication Data
Names: Howe, Susan, 1937– author.
Title: Debths / Susan Howe.
Description: New York, NY : New Directions Publishing, 2017.
Identifiers: LCCN 2017009786 | ISBN 9780811226851 (alk. paper)
Classification: LCC PS3558.O893 A6 2017 | DDC 811/.54—dc23
LC record available at https://lccn.loc.gov/2017009786

10 9 8 7 6 5 4 3 2

New Directions Books are published for James Laughlin
by New Directions Publishing Corporation
80 Eighth Avenue, New York 10011

CONTENTS

Foreword 9

Titian Air Vent 25

Tom Tit Tot 42

Periscope 101

Debths 129

childlinen scarf to encourage his obsequies where he'd check their debths in that mormon's thames, be questing and handsetl, hop, step and a deepend, with his berths in their toiling moil,

Finnegans Wake

FOREWORD

Going back! Going back!

"Little Sir Echo, how do you do? / Hello! (Hello!) Hello! (Hello!) / Little Sir Echo, we'll answer you / Hello! (Hello!) Hello! (Hello!) / Hello! (Hello!) Hello! (Hello!) / Won't you come over and play? (and play) / You're a nice little fellow / I know by your voice / But you're always so far away (away)."

Bing Crosby and the Music Maids (1939)

When I was eight my parents packed me off to Little Sir Echo Camp for Girls on Lake Armington in the foothills of New Hampshire co-founded and owned by Mary Hoisington and Margaret Conoboy ten years earlier. Apparently the women chose the name because of an echo that bounces off the surrounding White Mountains. An actual child may or may not fit parental fantasies. I hated the place. Most of all I dreaded riding classes and spent many nights praying I would be assigned the tired elderly horse with a creaking stomach for the next day's obligatory ride around the ring. On the one visiting day allowed per summer we rowed across the lake and picnicked on a secluded beach at the edge of a pine forest. I begged them to ransom me. But no. Around 4 pm they left for Boston, leaving me alone with my dread of being lost in the past; absent.

Show me affection as a small nonunderstanding person. Two people with covered lanterns stand on the brow of adjacent foothills. Watch them walking forward from folklore carrying tilted umbrellas. Faint whispers. Galaxy clusters. Telescopes also need to be tilted a little so that light traveling down an optical tube will come

into play. Calendar songs, family trees, broken branches, love songs, songs of captives, songs of robbers, songs around the campfire. "A tune beyond us, yet ourselves, // A tune upon the blue guitar." Chocorua is the highest mountain peak in New Hampshire. When Chief Chocorua leapt from its rocky summit to his death on the rocks below, war was in his heart. He put a curse on the land. "Last night at the end of night his starry head, / Like the head of fate, looked out in darkness." "Chocorua to Its Neighbor" is one of my favorite Wallace Stevens poems. Let's face things exactly as they are. He led a double life as a successful Surety and Fidelity Claims lawyer.

Speaking of the practice of law in relation to writing and second sight, *Peter Rugg, The Missing Man* is the first of "two tall tales" written by William Austin (1778–1841), a Massachusetts attorney. Austin presents its source as an old New England legend. An absent husband responsible for his own mysterious ruin is condemned to wander with his small daughter in a one-horse chair perpetually searching for Boston. In one of Nathaniel Hawthorne's lesser stories, "A Virtuoso's Collection," Rugg crops up with Peter Schlemilh's lost shadow and a famed New Hampshire gemstone. The precious jewel, said to sparkle (like a meteor) called for another Hawthorne story, "The Great Carbuncle of the White Mountains," this time inspired by an Amerindian fable from Saco, Maine: a manic Ruggian seeker wanders among mountains searching for the marvelous stone until the end of time. Some scholars say Austin's tall tale also foreshadows "Wakefield," which in its turn triggers Melville's "Bartleby the Scrivener." There are names under things and names inside names. "Poor [Rugg]! Little knowest thou thine own insignificance in this great world!"

Long ago people were afraid of mountains. The how and the why reflected in mystery plays and troll mythologies. Only art works are capable of transmitting chthonic echo-signals.

"Full many a glorious morning have I seen / Flatter the mountain tops with sovereign eye."

In the fall of 1889 Leonora Piper, the famous Boston medium, spent a week with William James and his wife at their house at Chocorua for discussions concerning various aspects of trance-phenomena including her trance-talk with "Phinuit" "a former native of this world." One afternoon they took a break from work and went fishing. Mrs. Piper caught the largest bass ever recorded in the lake.

There. Messages flow through clear lake water and yes, gravity pulls matter together to form a cosmic web. Even if this looks like the end of my Picnic at Lake Armington story the three of us are strung together like beads on a necklace. My fingers are too arthritic to work the little clasp.

"It's for the others"

The work in *Debths* was originally inspired by Paul Thek's retrospective called *Diver* in 2011. I have always been interested in folktales, magic, lost languages, riddles, coincidence, and missed connections. What struck me most was the way his later works, often painted swatches of color spread across sheets of newspaper with single words, phrases, or letters scribbled over the already doubled surface, transformed these so-called "art objects," into the epiphanies, riddles, spells and magical thinking I experienced one afternoon in the old Whitney Marcel Breuer building. I particularly loved the small bronze sculptures titled "The Personal Effects of the Pied Piper" scattered here and there. Shortly afterwards I spent a month as artist-in-residence at the Gardner Museum in Boston.

In 1903 Isabella Stewart Gardner personally installed her collection of over 2,500 objects (paintings, sculpture, furniture, textiles, drawings, tapestries, silver, ceramics, glassware, illuminated manuscripts, rare books, photographs, and letters from Europe, Asia, the Islamic world, and America) in a building modeled on the Palazzo Barbaro in Venice. (A view of the same palace from the Iron Bridge in Venice served as the model for Milly Theale's palazzo in *The Wings of the Dove*). When she died in 1924, Gardner endowed both building and grounds as a museum "for the education and enjoyment of the public forever" on the condition that her original arrangement of the objects in each gallery (or named room) would be kept just as she left them. Nothing was to be added, shifted, or sold. If her arrangements were disturbed, the property on what was once saltwater marshland in the Fenway Kenmore area—which she liked to call "Venice on the Fens"—including the art objects inside would be auctioned and the proceeds would go to Harvard University. The document was drafted and drawn up by her friend Professor John Chipman Gray, a member of the Harvard Law faculty and the author of *Restraints on the Alienation of Property*, *The Rule Against Perpetuities*, and *The Nature and Sources of the Law*.

Restraints (currently known as RAP) is encountered, often dreaded, by contemporary American law students. "Soon soon you will find the clue."

In 1999, the Museum directors felt it was time to "embark on a strategic planning process to plan for the future." They decided to build an addition to the original structure in order to relieve pressure on the aging interior spaces. In 2012 the added wing, designed by Renzo Piano—a soaring glass, steel, and copper-clad structure "crisp, light, and transparent, reminiscent of nautical design, and thus a deliberate foil to the closed 'plain brown wrapper' of the palace," opened to the public. Visitors now enter the original Willard T. Sears damp dimly lit late-Victorian faux-Venetian structure by passing through a minimalist glass and steel corridor.

At 10:15 one November morning a beam of sun slipped across the threshold. An echoing plash of water issuing from the mouths of stone dolphins blended with the scent of fresh red poinsettias, jade plants, and pyrocanthia in the atrium, while light flickering across ceramic floor tiles in the adjoining Spanish Cloister made them seem blue as the blue in Paul Thek's untitled synthetic polymer and gesso on newspaper (*Diver*) paintings.

Wandering through the inner rooms before and after visiting hours when whimsical combinations and odd analogies assume a second life, I began to think of Gardner as a pioneer American installation artist.

In the dimly lit Titian room Titian's *The Rape of Europa* (1561–1562) is displayed directly above a long swatch of pale green silk cut from her wedding gown designed by Charles Frederick Worth in 1860. "I am drinking myself drunk with Europa and then sitting for hours . . . ," she told her friend Bernard Berenson after he acquired it for her collection. I wonder if she was a drinker like my mother.

Isabella's little chair with its light blue slipcover is placed directly in front of *Christ carrying the Cross* (1505–1510), Circle of Giovanni Bellini. She has hung the portrait so that his tear-streaked face half shadowed by the angle of the wooden cross is aimed directly at Jupiter's savage eye in *Europa*. The Savior will not give up and be silent in true righteousness as a painted image.

The pages of A. B. Kempe's "Note to a Memoir on the Theory of Mathematical Form" are shattered to pieces. The filing cases are old, some of them shaky with loose covers and broken corners and sides. Mrs. Gardner didn't live to learn that in String Theory matter falls in. So the less said here concerning the ultimate nature of possible worlds and supermassive black holes in this our Godforsaken twenty-first century, the better.

Long, thinly transparent, slightly jaded gray window shades in the Raphael Room serve as a scrim or screen memory sheltering the goods in her faux-Venetian vessel from moving traffic and pedestrians. The walls are covered with elegant maroon fabric. Today a beam from the nuclear-hearted sun lights on a PLEASE DO NOT TOUCH sign before mercurially settling on *The Annunciation* by

Piermatteo d'Amelia (1450–1503), oil on wood, and then on Carlo Crivelli's *Saint George* (1470). Crivelli has depicted the saint as a thin teenager on a rearing horse with his sword joyfully lifted to slay the dragon. The horse's head jerks the other way. Its eye is distorted with terror.

Life / soul. Color, bearing, shape, size, magnitudo, figura, habitus corporis, anima

Stanza the sea. Earth the sea, *Fishman in Excelsis Table* (1970–71). Mixed media: wood, latex, wax, metal, paint, fabric, string, and Styrofoam, $29\frac{1}{2}$ x $35\frac{7}{16}$ x $94\frac{1}{8}$ in. (75 x 90 x 239 cm). My body is made of bones. In times of trouble and perplexity I am able to bend my limbs and stretch myself into a Forsaken Merman but Oh, little school chair with Manhattan cityscape hung at child's-eye level I wish I were young again. If I had only known earlier that indeterminacy involves all of life I might fathom the luminous story surrounding all things noumenal.

The Portrait of a Lady in Black (1590s), once attributed to Jacobo Tintoretto (1518–1594) and later to his son Domenico, is at the top of the third floor landing just to the right of the Veronese Room entrance. According to the guidebook, Tintoretto's portrait of a Venetian woman is a glorification of wealth and station rather than a character study. More care is focused on the contrast between decorative details of jewels, lace, and curtain than on the roughly defined yet vividly lit landscape seen to the upper right. The sitter remains a cipher, her personality as much as her identity a mystery.

How do you match people as they seem on the surface with who they are actually are? I assume she is a widow because her clothes are black.

We have so little time in the distant present. Echo cannot stop reflecting the original enchantment of the good mother beyond representation, her eye of nature absorbed in surface azure of poise and balance, rhythmic rise and fall of words, their deep ecology and threads of Divinity. Hush be quiet deep-green pagan marvels. You see the double evidence—as the place, the time, the fashion of other lives determined by grounds outside our power which leaves the good mother absorbed in you here on the landing in peace and plenty. I try as hard as I can to wish myself into your presence through art foreshadowing life after death for some notes of promise that the aesthetic holds out or holds on to an idea of the formal rigors of poetry as light and impulse. Then the free cause of expression may return to the morality of things I want to remember as first things last. Gardner has placed the painting high on the east wall in the center of an older tapestry resembling a wishing carpet, all swirls of plants and people gesturing. The embroidered damask serves as a double frame. Our Lady of the Labyrinth, captured in oscillating memory folds of simple household affections exhibits, her glistening necklace armor.

Standing here in early evening when the viewers are leaving and the lights are dimmed I remember Mary (Minny) Temple's personal letters to John Chipman Gray, and Henry James' splendidly written passages in *The Wings of the Dove* when Milly Theale,

Minny's fictional double, wandering through one of the great gilded chambers of Matcham, sees herself mirrored in Bronzino's *Portrait of a Woman*. "The lady in question, at all events, with her slightly Michael-angelesque squareness, her eyes of other days, her full lips, her long neck, her recorded jewels, her brocaded and wasted reds, was a very great personage—only unaccompanied by a joy. And she was dead, dead, dead."

It's late November. Fallen oak and maple leaves on the sidewalk outside are bound to childhood landscape memories filtered through my mother who never stopped harping on the cruel ugliness of Boston as compared to Dublin's fair city. For me there are two alternatives: either swallow or break free

The Rule Against Perpetuities resembles a postmodern labyrinth in need of a golden thread. Some poets and lawyers keep trying, some groping through intricate passages half-paralyzed, never do. John Gray stands in for my father. As life rushes by we do our best with the nerves we inherit. The guards at the entrance are watching so we won't get away with anything.

Epistolary Correspondences.
Before I was sent to Little Sir Echo I had an imaginary friend who lived in our Buffalo mailbox. His name was Mr. Bickle. When we moved to Cambridge he vanished as transitional objects tend to do although his name lives on as a family anecdote.

Strange that one half-suffocated picnic in the course of life can disappear into Lake Armington's hanging rock echo portals. Until the replication of love prevails in art and *Periscope*—one of Paul Thek's late "picture-light" paintings, bubbles up from puddle blue depths

So many things happen by bringing to light what has long been hidden. Lilting betwixt and between. Between what? Oh everything. Take your microphone. Cross your voice with the ocean.

I'm here, I'm still American

Control

Those months beside Lake Armington may have influenced an adult obsession with early American Captivity Narratives. Mary Rowlandson's *The Sovereignty & Goodness of God, Together, with the Faithfulness of His Promises Displayed* ... was published in Boston in 1682. She was taken captive in an Amerindian raid on Lancaster, Massachusetts during what came to be known as King Philip's (Metacomet) War and went missing with three of her children. "If God be gone our Guard is gone." She wasn't frozen like a twig in an ice storm. She didn't snap.

If the shoe pinches take it off. Twenty "Removes" from "civilization" in another space of inclusion or non inclusion you may think you slip from time but on second sight the rules are more stringent in terms of giving yourself up and crossing back. This Mary was ransomed home to her family and sheets of parchment open to skeleton clauses. Paper is stationary, unlike a wandering ghost it survives being rag or bark. Oh—I've forgotten about eating. Spitting things out there has to be some bleed-through. Think of coming to second life but only in waves

Whispering red herrings

"Can we walk together without the table?" Probably not. When writing personal letters I have sometimes gone too far. Maybe belief and trust in another's love is an obsessional desire to control a wayward eyewitness. I could go on and on about the origins of transference via H. D. and *The Sword Went Out to Sea* but a foreword is a like a fish tank so there isn't room here for leaping dolphins, solo séances, hallucinatory visions, dead pilots, the atomic bomb, nervous breakdowns, the Küsnacht clinic March–November 1946.

Sigh sough rough wind world war.

Philological wilderness encounters.

"Secret Paintings / the / object of which is not / to be seen // He made a secret out / of what no one / wanted anyway" is a motto found in one of Thek's diaries.

Goodbye goodbye *Portrait of a Lady in Black* sheltering sound eye of Europe my imagination of Europe in your everlastingly dim spot on the third floor landing. The last time I looked you seemed to be hoping for something. Stormy landscape out the window to your left.

The soul appears or occurs as something we feel compelled to live into or to move toward as if it were there floating a little apart and at an angle or

Rattling the door with a sound of wailing and lamentation

We can shift attention from here to there during the course of
a singular ocular fixation.

"Milly spoke with her eyes again on her painted sister's"

All the eyes in all the paintings

Alberti's winged-eye emblem

Hyperacute part of the retina. the fovea

restless eye

Cognitive focus of "attention"

Small head and torso of a Silenus with wineskin

Graeco Roman

Motif of variation of statues of Eros carrying an amphora

Child satyrs holding wine skins

The lure of Bog-Latin, Shelta and Bēarlagair na Sāer, Ogham, and cryptology may feel superannuated or fatally picturesque to some, but I treasure my edition of *The Secret Languages of Ireland* by the archaeologist R. A. Stewart Macalister. It's reprinted by Craobh Books (Armagh, 1997) and has a paper over board cover, a plain light blue jacket with text normally reserved for the inside flap in simple serif typeface on the front, so the effect is both dryly pedagogical and rebellious. According to Macalister the work is based on a random collection of loose sheets, letters, manuscript notebooks, scraps of paper, dictionary slips, "relics of the industry of the late lamented John Sampson, known to all as one of the greatest of the world's authorities on the Gypsies." *Secret Languages* is wonderfully littered with etymological particulars, diacritical characters, hieroglyphs, wordlists, oblique slashes.

Sometimes I think of "Tom Tit Tot" and "Debths" as collaged essays on the last poems of William Butler Yeats, the poet I loved first.

~~I thought that old old age might show~~
grow old to show
I ~~thought I could show me~~ what
What
~~That line~~‸~~of~~ Robert Browng ment
'An old hunter talking with gods'
But now
~~But o my god~~ I am not content

~~dream~~
~~rem~~[?~~n~~]~~ent~~

Content

New Poems was the last collection published in Yeats's lifetime. I enjoy facsimile editions (such as the Cornell *New Poems: Manuscript Materials*) of poets whose manuscripts have a strong visual component.

What interests me most isn't the photographed handwritten original on the even numbered side but the facing typographical transcription on the odd. These doggedly Quixotic efforts at conversion are a declaration of faith. The textual scholar hopes, through successive processes of revision, to draw out something that resists articulated shuffling. Secret connections among artifacts are audible and visible and yet hidden until you take a leap—overwriting signified by a vertical brace—superimposed letters with others underneath—sometimes empty brackets signify a tear or a worn place. It's the mystery of strong music in the soul. Our eyes see what is outside in the landscape in the form of words on paper but *inside,* a slash or mark wells up from a deeper place where music before counting hails from.

                                        the
[Search the [?cliff] sides & find ~~these~~ three

~~But then in joy~~
~~When all is broken~~
                        all may
Thoug all be broken. & yet be whole
~~Rock~~ [?~~minds~~]~~, if can find these three,~~
~~If you be~~
Old rocky face if you can find the three
                        a   a
That can perfect ~~the~~ work, ~~the~~ life the soul,

Hnuy illa nyha, majah Yahoo
"Strike the rock," says the Piper, "and tears will come out." "Remember I have been here for an endless number of years always keeping up with laggards. These instructions are not to be whinnied around Boston."

TITIAN AIR VENT

A work of art is a world of signs, at least to the poet's
nursery bookshelf sheltered behind the artist's ear.
I recall each little motto howling its ins and outs
to those of us who might as well be on the moon
illu illu illu

Beacon

A tiny artificial theater of the world. I am here to slay the dragon in the ready-made name of an earlier Susan. While there is still time do you know anything about my watch being stopped? Put your hand over my eyes and say I have got it in my mind.

Ceramic, plaster, laquer, newspaper

Footprint

Certain bronze elements found among the Pied Piper's personal effects have been moved from one exhibition room to another. Here are messages. "The Face of God." "Dust," "Time is a river." Props and other disinherited paraphernalia are never enough.

I have to go in and catch my breath

Electric bulb

It's a manic condition; barbaric conceptions of an "other self" sawing away our finite future as we approach the laws which govern clutter; leaving at death to return no more although fitfully visiting old haunts with the aid of metal, clay, gouache, glass, glue

Odysseus Creeping Forward during the Theft of the Palladium

"If you want to know what the law used to be, go to such an one of his colleagues; if you want to know what it is going to be, go to such another; if you want to know what the law ought to be, go to a third; but if you happen to want to know what the law is, go to Gray."

John Chipman Gray and the *Rule Against Perpetuities*

Something more ancient than what you remember or may not

remember moved me to lean on you. Because of all the dead.

I can't.

My cry is in the frost

Mary Temple. Present as absent.

The Dutch Room, Saint Patrick's Day, March 18th, 1990.

You can't fool a regular boarder, as Mr. Holmes would say.

Morse Code, army flag signal, plaster

Ellen Sturgis Hooper. 1812–1848.

Thanks to Boston here is a poem.

"I slept, and dreamed that life was beauty

I woke and found that life was duty

Was thy dream then a shadowy lie?

Toil on poor heart, unceasingly. . . ."

Glass, plasticine, dried flowers, foliage

Te turo turo

Running footsteps. Interlete te interlute. Ages have passed. A bell of the Chou Dynasty is in my hands. Goodbye for the present. I seem to go back to things that do not belong to me. Call when you get depressed. There are those of us at a distance who may have seemed to drop out of touch but never really did

Mary Howitt. 1799–1888

Oh for some old Mystery

Something we could not know—

Something we could not fathom—

As it was long time ago.

Yamuna river map, spreadsheet, riverbed

Eme ede ege edu elu

Peter Rugg with child, horse, and open chair. “Is this the way to Boston?”

Eye piece, prism, Euryscope, Platiscope

Perpetuities

Boston shifts with the winds and plays with the compass.

We are oathbound we cannot stop, so hush little chair

with light blue slipcover

Reliquary, trellis cross-grid, shoelace, comma

For what Porpoise

My body is made of bones. In times of trouble and perplexity I can bend my limbs and stretch half fish half Fishman in Excelsis. A luminous aura surrounds all things noumenal. No need for money money money

Believe me I am not rubbish

Lattice Phonesis

This variagated fabric band hints at what waking point, within itself and upon itself, a work of art is nourished and multiplied through subliminal abecedarian recollection

Antique Mirror

Etce ce Tera. Forgotn quiet all. Nobody grows old and crafty

here in middle air together. Long ago ice wraith foliage.

I had such fren

Our mother of puddled images fading away into deep blue
polymer.
        Seaweed, nets, shells, fish, feathers

TOM TIT TOT

ι ι ι $\overline{\epsilon_1\ \varphi_1}(\epsilon_1, x)$. ue,
&c.) $\varphi\ n\ ([\epsilon], x)$

combats of the playground

"they are crowded with o
and reworkings" crowde
little monuments of paint
inch a space of scrutiny ar
Scattered marks and loop
off words from images twi
from their original source
history scattered to the fou
of a page it was *you* playin
There are those of us who i
[illegible]
~~Oh the grows, leaf sown~~
^

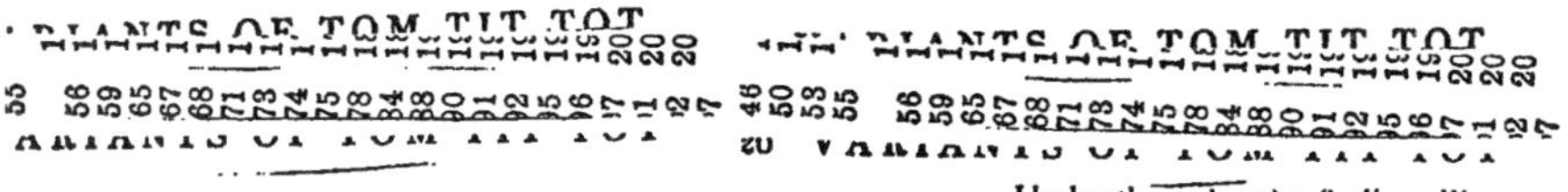

~~Under~~ the cobwebs & ~~dim villages~~

IANTS OF TOM TIT TOT

46 50 53 55 56 59 65 67 68 71 73 74 75 78 84 88 90 91 92 95 96 97

Serch [?] [?out] thes three to know

Or else betwe the pole cat & the owl

μοελυκτα,

"Υια γ' ιππευει καπυροῖς απταις

TANGIBLE THINGS
DIFFUSION OF

TANGIBLE THINGS

FUSION OF

Out of a stark oblivion ~~disenter~~

Constrained, ~~[illegible]~~, barred bent & unbent

[ἀφραδίαισιν ἐπεὶ ὄπιν, [illegible] of wood

[the], to thee, 239.
them, for themsel'
[t]her-till, thithe:
therto, to that en'
[thester], darknes
thinge, *pl.* things,
tho, then, 115.
tholed, suffered, 1
thought, it seeme
threw, crowded, !
thronge[s], presse
throw, through, '
[tigh]t, went, 420
till, to, 394.
tipen, fall, 194.
to, *adv.* too, 87.
to, *prep.* in additi
[traystly], faithf
treystr.

'Tell us our names,
of the underworld is vo

…n they before were;
ouer the hills with

~~ou~~ ~~ld old~~

ɔld to

& an

did ~~whether~~ we spok

[illegible] for euer! Amen.

— ilent sandal'd ~~Duncers)~~ pay our ⟨defter⟩ court

~~deft — homage pay our silent court~~

w[a] a wa d d wa wa wa wa wa wa wa wa wa wa

~~Or in our rude~~ a Or
Or ~~at the silent~~ haply
Or. haply.

~~because~~ I stay quiet

e,
nd
vay,
adr
r[ed
ræ
nt, li
ppet
re, w
rned
rped
rran
ry, c
sts, t
xen,
yte, v

~~The Spirit lifting, his strong arm hath sworn~~

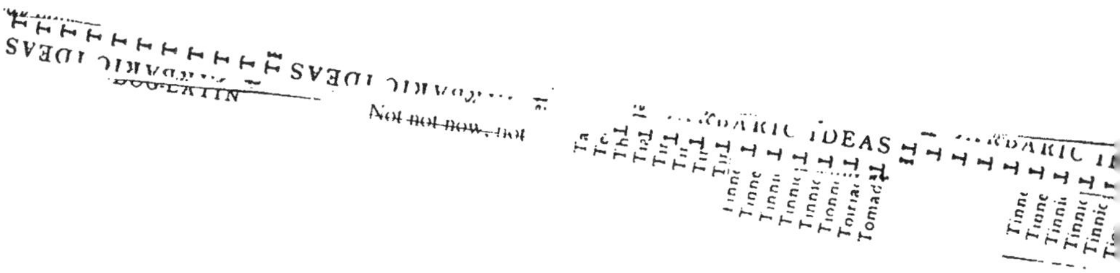
Not not now, not
IDEAS

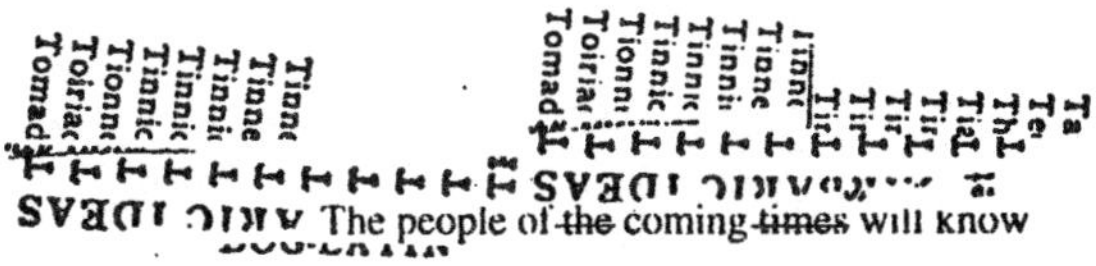
The people of ~~the~~ coming ~~times~~ will know

:hild cry from within a mountain, while
ss quieted it with these words, 'Hush,
-morrow comes thy father, Wind and
home, bringing

rushd ~~I have rushd~~

-IC IDEAS ABOUT NAMES

ɔaptism,[1] an importance whi

less pr·:cise reasons, by rustics ich is

'children never thrive till th' who

and that the night air thril ey 're

: homeless souls of the unbapt ls to

BARBARIC IDEAS ABOUT NA

The rymes I have made ~~that I~~

hold, mast, sail, blocks, paddles,
and hull each putting the same
sailor, the wind, the river, and the
chiming in, and the Rubric ending

May And build your judgemnt citing upon

DA TOD UND LEBEN

'Forgetng human words' — fill out fac

Breme birds on the boughes busilye
& all the wild in the wood winlye the
Kings kneeled on their knees, knowing
& all the princes in the presse, & the pr
and their heads covered with linnen: but th
shaven, which were the terrene stars of the gc
ıands instruments of brasse, silver and gold, ı

INTRODUCTI

& the crowne on her head
With a scepter sett in her
Thus louelye to looke vpon
Merry were the meanye of
Blyth bearnes of blee, brigh
Dallyance & Disport, [two]
With all beawtye [&] blisse,
There was minstrelsye made
Who-soe had craft or cuning
we did whether we spoke or sang

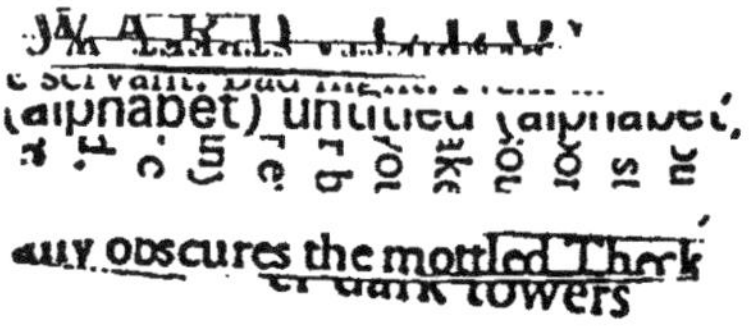
(alphabet) untitled (alphabet,
obscures the mottled
dark towers

…ing by laying excessive stress on
zaging in true explication that allows for an
Uncle Tom's cabin, dinosaurs, turtles, udge
cherries and prunes set in each case on s. ho
a thin monochrome ground that only
partially obscures the news paper grid
mottled Theck blue terrace in distance
ids its readers 'See Edgar's song in

A document, the parasitic
nvolve a structure of layer
age placed on top of anoth
om its other, as if to infinit

PORTABLE OCEAN

and loop
ords from images twi
their original source
ory scattered to the fou
page it was *you* playir
re are those of us wh
wilša? Axa
wilša ga mi (in) grit'
wilša('s) kam

~~← haply → pay our~~
~~in deft homage pay our silent court~~
(defter) court

Lost, lost as secret on the side of
others looking back as specimens
Melancholically alive in prison ho
Polaroids,and reproduction of la
Many fish. Elephants, a zebra, so
[illegible]

what secret place his heart is hidden. He tells her that it is in an egg in a duck swimming in a well in a church on an island, all which she straightway repeats to her true love who has stolen into the castle to rescue her. With the aid of a number of helpful animals, a common

ie'll
't, I
'hat
five
rays
got
ven
ate,
the
gan
r if
say
1.
kes
ere
ool.
in
if

ıikin's territory either with his life
nder of his wife. The count ple
›n, and the dwarf so far modifies hi
agree that if within a month the
›t find out his name, she is to be his.
ing the count to the forest bound
an ancient fir-tree, it is bargained t
' will there await the countess, wh
three crosses, three times
lovely valley, and, seeing a tiny house
WOODSLIFFERCOUNTERCLATTER

the count to the foresunds where
ancient fir-tree, it is baed that the
ill there await the coun who shall
ee guesses three times, nir all. The
xpires, and she then rs to the
is to make her first rouf guesses,
e names, 'Janne,' 'Fichtel 'Fohre.'
rf shrieks with merrimover her
goodbye for the present.

her with invisible mi
and raiom Tippe her i
the liviissiles, hı she
And alFamily, bite is
cannot f is drivdher nai
that, shı manife be in
sarcasm me, forff is err
is given their entrap
name,—aploynich she
with fits of laughter.
her most at night, cor
over her bed-head, whi
and then, being a goc
chapters and verses fr
them away. And alth

ere nitwit, who wasted precious parchment
WOODSLIPPERCOUNTERCLATTER
WOODSLIPPERCOUNTERCLATTER
WOODSLIPPERCOUNTERCLATTER

.n certain Shrouds that
ne and were gone. He lean
though to meditate on wo

Secret Painting

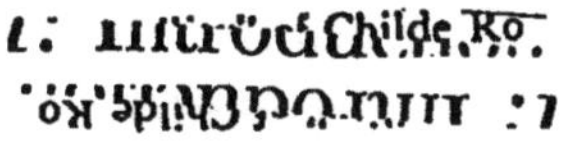
Childe Ro.

rning finish my play. Triumphant,
erpiece. That night, sleeping draft,
. Next morning begin ballad about
nt. Bad night. Next morning finish
nt; believe I have written a master-
each. Will take a whole Broadside
ect my wife's suggestions for nex
over press. She explains that my
ıcapable of facing practical life. Ill
Good night. Then on Wednesday
ınd decide to do no serious worl
and this morning perfectly well
INCIDENTAL FEATURES
Move with "green radiance"

~~Knowing that s~~

~~Though~~ And the play but half done

In the whole world. The te
Points to the shipman thus t
He strikes on, only when

ı the tower with the bell ringing al
the speaker has left the dark wood:
ight walk out

hroud that seemed to ha

ong those bird-like things

undle of linen. Shrouds b

Till Me Wh An In As The An The Me The

Coleridge walked with me to

standing in the room he kisse

'Almost forgets human words' ~~he said~~

To put

Spinoza's face in the title-page.

To ~~judge me do~~

?] ~~the Shallows of~~ his eagerness to steer ott
ιad gone on refining and refining on the
ıad left him, no nature at all, and instead of
.o the mind, virtually excluding the divine
' ascribed to, and the perpetual substitution
ng the idea of God Natureless, and Nature
urging the fiends to bar the gates. Now that sl

prisoned within the outline of any single

live the *heart* in the *head*; gave me an i

ent, that all the products of the mere *refle*

he rattling twigs and sprays in winter,

… If they were too often a moving clou

ys a pillar of fire throughout the night, d

: of doubt, and enabled me to skirt, with

~~What matter, u hat mattr,~~ what mattr)ZA, ma

The berries of the half up-rooted ash

:e beings and God.

Every individual thing, or everything cannot exist or be conditioned to act, by another cause other than itself, whi and likewise this cause cannot in its t conditioned for existence and action l conditioned existence, and so on to in:

The gentle Spirits of the place
Them oft the

were always a pillar of fire throughout the nigh
wilderness of doubt, and enabled me to skirt, v
utter unbelief. That the system is capable of
PANTHEISM, I well know. The ETHICS of SPINOZA,
at no time could I believe, that *in itself* and *essen*
THE NAME AND THE SOUL.

was dread ~~has is~~

sing what ~~is~~ lost & ~~hate~~ what is ^ won

ndistinct, yet stirring and working

ctive faculty partook of DEATH, and

into which the sap was yet to be

d of smoke to me by day, yet they

uring my wanderings through the

out crossing, the sandv deserts of

ng converted into an irreligious

be an instance. But

That tremble in the stream below—

Holy for euer! Amen.
ilent sandal'd ~~Dancers)~~ pay our ⟨defter⟩ court
~~deft —— homage pay our silent court~~
ɔck. And long may it
~~us~~ if only we are at
:laim as we ~~pass~~ sail
:e a Sea-mark for us

…ing by laying excessive stress on
gaging in true explication that allows for an
changes our apprehension of the Last Judge
pistle to the Corinthians, clothing does, ho
…ης τὼς ὤπερ αι … the Shrouds in Yeats's poem
οὐδ' ἀμῶς ἐπ· δοκεῖ τ' … sometime y
flamy,

rs, whose garments glistered a
re puro luminosi']. The womer
eads covered with linnen: but
ich were the terrene stars of the
uments of brasse, silver and gol
oi ia ua[sic] *ae*

. manifests the aspect of all go   om
uniformis' (Apuleius 1989: ii. 2
ne. which expresses the synchr   —
omforted'; its symbolic apprehe   ld
n of letting linen fall and taking   to

first beheld thy ideal vibes with wondrous
eye serene

(seek/ search
Some

the sailor, the wind, the river,

they before were;

question, over the hills with

river-banks chiming in, and the rubric ending

all the white scarfed riders
rying that shall be tomorro

blue terrace in distance

aim his hopes and fears about a life's wor
n makes the earlier poet speak with alt
vning's 'Childe Roland to the Dark Tower (

aph I For pastime in the dusty thoroughfare

ory and memory, wchosen
ıd Childe Roland is ammer
his source in Shakesp of ar
allegorical story to fiw frui
whose branches flashed the on
cold, amid the woods, the th
ıtside the [illegible] carri
[illegible] With c

fears about a life's work
er poet speak with alter
and to the Dark Tower C
drama that

[illegible]

the dusty thoroughfare
written his own epitaph
ns. in the poem that sh
the witch's bargain being

ient within us today. Like Au
t-past, present-present, and
logue, my tropological read
f 'The Black Tower'. At the e
find that it begins within
~~Though~~ And the play but half done
wn the spiral stair? Yeats's po
ction and history: it is vivif

dwarf will there await the countess, who shall

stood an ancient fir-tree, it is bargained that the

dwarf will there await the countess, who shall

handle touch and spa
those that crosse Tol
vhat the panther dan
ı a host of furious fa
reof I am commandı
ı a burning spear anc
ıe wilderness I wand
knight of ghostes an
ımon'd am to tourne

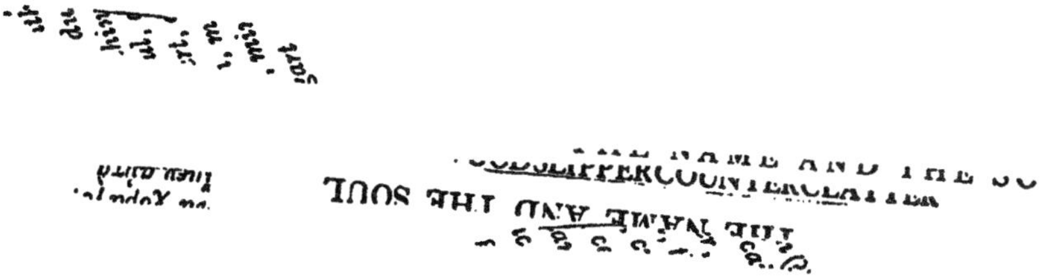

but, one day, as t
a wild horse in th
at him, and by mis
with the iron bit,
vanished.[1]

er's edges. The par-
n underneath, half
:hance for any unity
d, dust and puddle,
pposition in its most
, and yet all will be
TTLE above eye-
l if not a little below

PERISCOPE

God's foot upon the treadle of the loom

Moby-Dick

Closed book who stole
who away do brackets
signify emptiness was
it a rift in experience

Mackerel and porpoise
was this the last of us

These tallied scraps float

like glass skiffs quietly for

love or pity and all that

What an idea in such a time

as ours Pip among Pleiads

Mystical accidentalism for
sound-hemmed naught in
night's botanical glossary

Over unnamed cycles see
the rich on that rust heap

Once when the real world
was our world in its nature
to mind our would world
Threshold word little hinge
hope of bewilderment its
parchment memory sign

Each word may be six six

razzle rungs it may be two

places at once in the old

secret escapades a vault

benediction for one lucky

one under thimble thumb

Cobble on downward path
long story renegade with
silver money in latch box

Plaint when then was then
at the lief end of ciphers

Cross counterclockwise via
cobbled childhood juvenilia
to hobbled monosandalism

Choose one rugged raggedy
quatrain its puppet pattern

A coverlet has drifted down

in double compass with sled

loom as if it were patterned

Many shuttles many treadles

That beam was only a straw

So long as one fact stands
isolated and strange one
fact supported by no fact

Woodslippercounterclatter
I can spin straw by myself

If to sense you are

alive is pleasant itself

or can be nearly so—

If I knew what it is

I'd show it—but no

What I lack is myself

Come lie down on my shadow

Being infinitely self-conscious

I sold your shadow for you too

Let's let bygones be bygones

Dust to dust we barely reach

You sit in our tent of belief

and ask what to do with it

Faithful first then frivolous

Half scientific but good at

guessing by sensation you

look at a flame is it orange

within you or without you

In another poem I'm in a
perfectly black room with
my eyes directed on this
sheet of paper to make a
long story short I will tell
Baba Yaga in her tinsel hut
to heal your hobble foot

Hut running on chicken legs
Achilles has his heel what’s
left to a thirdhand sightseer

Caves and rivers imagine
having to bury yourself over
and over knock on wood

Telling the story of a man
who is responsible for his
own ruin and is inexplicably
condemned to wander in
a one-horse chair eternally
around Boston from which
historical song he himself
cannot free himself with a
wave of his hand whither—

Dusk friars carrying tapers blow
farewell kisses to Peter Rugg our
missing man but what's the use

he's skipping across roof tops
Let's be human we can't carry
the Galoshes of Fortune home

In the old days I used to sit
up late till an owl appeared
Negative infinity melodrama

I shall never forget you half-
way owl shadow marauder
How you flew over and over

To stagger and fall to the
nether side of the hut never
to stand with your back to
the forest because the hut
when it wants to allegedly
rushes this way then that
Do you hear the clock lock
Just wait till I turn back—

When stars are not so faint
and new astronomers assign
numbers one may count one
other and each secretly jot
down in units and tenths for
photometrics other instant
infinitesimal arc predicates
A nearest faint ghost alias—

Unseen in canoe or cut glass
skiff scudding past centuries
on another map kept secret

from earth moon vision each
reflecting an end point where
is will remain as is etcetera

Setting sun then Lethe where
ever fabled swan-white Helios
in our own time underground

In this second place we think
we only think we think though
our ghosts appear in mirrors

If you remember cosmology
there is nothing to stop time
running all the way to zero

Lying up or even lying down
I will just wiggle my hand to
remind you I was timorous

A day without yesterday

Mackerel sky over Boston

See tossing waves at ice

font doorstep nonfiction

prosepoem my icicle hair

This side I will show miniature
network entanglements comma
Blessings full stop yours very

half-hesitation semi-colon semi-
colon yes the sea lies about us
Our tininess on earth as such

These quiet stars each free
intelligence sealed from us
Days and hours are blinds

These screens these means
each new extreme outvies
each quickening after after

After the millennium a little
before at brink at the brink

Humming octaves with wild
trills of magic and symbolic
logic a not-being-in-the-no

DEBTHS

[illegible]
Upon the frontier of

Religious Musi

~~whose first beheld th Ideal tribes~~

~~fibre~~

Infant

~~Pressing on his stepses close bel~~

.*long* ; ă, ĕ, ĭ, ŏ, ŭ, y̆, *short* ; ạ, ẹ, ị, ọ, ụ, ỵ,

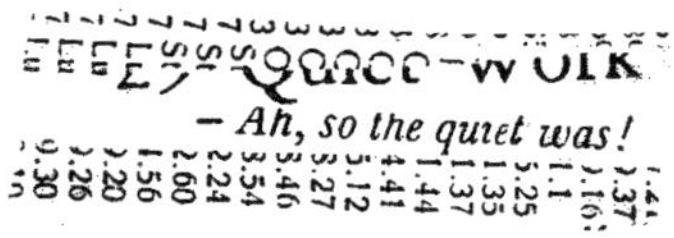
– Ah, so the quiet was!

ŏ mў Soul ănd Rĕtūrn

[?Whv/?Which] the had lack

←quality:→

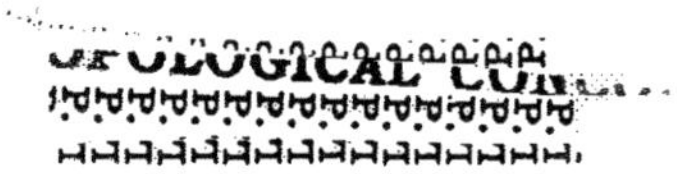
LOGICAL

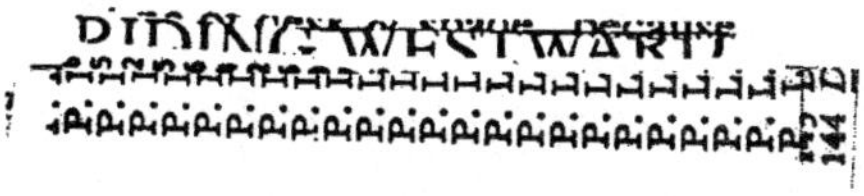

078 Nothing
078 Nothing
082 Nothing
082 Nothing
083 Nothing
1103 Nothing
1104 Nothing
1104 Nothing
1111 Nothing
1111 Nothing
1112 Nothing 3
1113 Nothing 3
1119 Nothing 3
1126 Nothing 4

1141 Nothing 4
1147 Nothing 5
1148 Nothing 5
1148 Nothing 5
1152 Nothing 5
1153 Nothing 5
1154 Nothing 5
1160 Nothing 5
1160 Nothing 5

1160 Nothing 5
1175 Diarmuid 1
1180 Diarmuid 1

1181 Diarmuid 1
1184 Diarmuid 1
1184 Diarmuid 1
1187 Diarmuid 1
1189 Diarmuid 2

leaves to all the creatures meanest, highest, to all the meanest

ur Death, the TREE OF KNOWLEDGE, gi

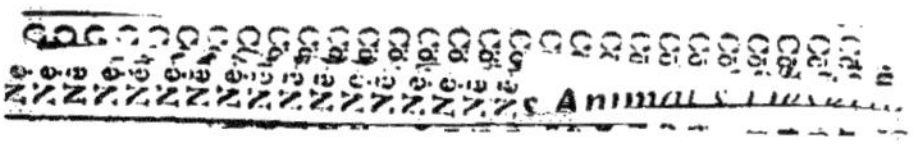

Upon the frontier of unimaged night

Nigl Nigl Nigl Nigl Nigl Nigl Nigl Nigl Nigl Nigl Nigl Nigl Nigl Nigl Nigh Ni-g Nig- Ni-h Nill Nim Nim Nim Nim Nin Nine Nine Nine Nine Nine Nine Nine Nine Nine Nin'n Ninth Ninth Nip, v

dĭvīdduŏŏus āll, āll rūshĭng

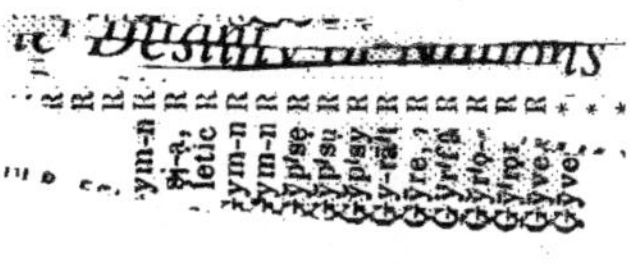

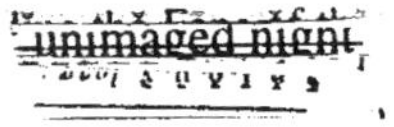
unimaged

ĭts wātĕrs ăbrēăst:

~~pull to~~